Pray Now
2009

Daily Devotions for the Year 2009

Pray Now
2009

Daily Devotions for the Year 2009

Published on behalf of the
OFFICE FOR WORSHIP AND DOCTRINE,
MISSION AND DISCIPLESHIP COUNCIL,
THE CHURCH OF SCOTLAND

SAINT ANDREW PRESS
Edinburgh

First published in 2008 by
SAINT ANDREW PRESS
121 George Street, Edinburgh EH2 4YN

Copyright © Office for Worship and Doctrine, Mission and Discipleship Council, the Church of Scotland, 2008

ISBN 978 0 86153 388 6

British Library Cataloguing in Publication Data
A catalogue record for this book is available from the British Library

It is the Publisher's policy to only use papers that are natural and recyclable and that have been manufactured from timber grown in renewable, properly managed forests. All of the manufacturing processes of the papers are expected to conform to the environmental regulations of the country of origin.

Typeset by Waverley Typesetters, Fakenham
Manufactured in Spain by Associated Agencies

Contents

Preface   ix

Using this Book and CD   xi

Hospitable

Day 1   HOME   4
Day 2   GARDENS   6
Day 3   WORK   8
Day 4   REST   10
Day 5   NOISE   12
Day 6   ARTIFICIAL   14
Day 7   TREES   16

Sky

Day 8   STARS   20
Day 9   RAINBOW   22
Day 10   ECLIPSE   24
Day 11   LIGHTNING   26
Day 12   HORIZON   28
Day 13   CLOUDS   30

Alienating

Day 14   BARRENNESS   34
Day 15   MIST/FOG   36
Day 16   LONELY PLACE   38
Day 17   VOID   40
Day 18   CROWDED   42
Day 19   DEPTHS   44

Elemental

Day 20   RAIN   48

Day 21   EBB AND FLOW   50

Day 22   WIND   52

Day 23   FLOOD   54

Day 24   HURRICANE   56

Day 25   FIRE   58

Day 26   STORMS   60

Perceived

Day 27   HEIGHT   64

Day 28   MYSTERY   66

Day 29   OPEN/CLOSED   68

Day 30   SURFACE   70

Day 31   SACRED EARTH   72

Serving Overseas   74

Acknowledgements   75

Preface

Daily prayer is as crucial to our spiritual life as water is to our physical. At times, however, many find the discipline of daily prayer difficult; there are many distractions, many other things to do. How can we focus our thoughts for this time of prayer?

For years, *Pray Now* has proved to be an invaluable resource to a large number of people in their daily prayer life. *Pray Now* helps us to focus our thoughts by offering reflection, activities, Bible readings and prayers.

The 2009 theme, 'The Environment', is one which is particularly relevant for all our lives. The environment is that which surrounds our lives: noise and quietness, crowds and solitude, home and work, built and natural. The theme reminds us that we are part of, and we relate to, the world and the people around us in many different ways. The environment in which we live influences us as we influence it. It was the poet John Donne who wrote that no-one is an island entire of itself. The reflections, readings and prayers in the pages that follow lead us to reflect prayerfully on the different environments in which we live, of which we are all part.

May you find in these pages a rich and valuable resource for your daily prayer life.

REV. ALAN D. BIRSS
Convener
Worship and Doctrine Task Group
of the Mission and Discipleship Council
2008

Using this Book and CD

Wherever we go, whatever we do, the environment has a profound effect on our lives. The Pray Now Group have this year written daily prayers to reflect on a world where climate change, international conflict and disasters are keenly sensed and communicated by the global community. We also celebrate the beauty and power of the natural world, and the role of people in God's creation. The prayers are offered to readers as a way to create an environment of devotion within Christian living.

Once again, there is a CD to complement the contents of the book. The CD has five tracks, each introducing a different theme on the environment, followed by a reading of one of the daily prayers from that section in the book. You have the option of using the book consistently throughout the month and the CD from time to time, or of alternating the use of both mediums on different days depending on time available and indeed the circumstances of readers or listeners.

The 31-day format gives structure and pattern to the month for those who like to move through Day 1 to Day 31 in a natural progression. You may wish to choose a prayer from one of the five sections, using a different section each day, or you may just prefer to dip in and out of the book. Whatever is most helpful to you is recommended. We hope, however, whether you are sitting quietly in your favourite chair in the house, or at your desk at work, or listening in the car or kitchen, at home or on holiday, through using *Pray Now* the variety of environments we find ourselves in and God's voice within them will be understood and appreciated in a deeper, enriching way.

GAYLE TAYLOR
Convener of the Pray Now *Group*

Days of the Month

Hospitable

In the beginning God created the Garden of Eden to house the life made in his image. People have been creating gardens ever since. Over the ages, what we call a 'home' has changed in terms of structures and internal fittings but the function remains the same: a place of reassuring familiarity and security that whispers 'you belong!'

It is good to build or discover spaces where we feel wrapped in welcome. In Jesus' ministry, we know he found hospitality in the homes of Martha and Mary and of Zacchaeus. The noisy market place, the quiet mountainside and the busy lakeside were all places where Jesus found space to teach and to heal.

Can we define absolutely every set of surrounding as either 'hospitable' or 'inhospitable'? Picture Golgotha, 'the place of the skull'. Can you imagine anywhere less hospitable? Yet on the cross, we are shown the act of ultimate hospitality – Jesus with his arms outstretched welcoming us into the grace of a forgiving God.

Maybe the hospitableness of any place depends simply on what we do there.

HOME

Lord, whenever I see a sign,
'God bless this house'
I think of the one
over Norma's hospital bed.
Visiting, I would bend down,
kiss her paper-thin cheek,
and grasping my hand,
she would say, 'Welcome,'
'I'm sure they'll get you a cup of tea
if you would like.'

Hospitable to the end,
that was her!

And I would wonder
at the small fragile frame,
tortuously twisted in Spina Bifida
that housed
such a beautiful soul:
a body so closed and a heart so open.
Friend or stranger,
morning, noon or night,
there was always room
at Norma's council flat
for sharing food and conversation.
Her interest and concern for the other
was like a warm wrapping.

Lord, God,
build Your home in me too
that I may offer myself
as home to others
ready to share myself and my resources.

Readings

Ruth 1:6–18	*Ruth's home is now with her mother-in-law*
Psalm 127	*God's blessings in the home*
Luke 19:1–10	*Jesus goes to Zacchaeus's home*
John 19:25–7	*John takes Jesus' mother into his home*
Acts 16:11–15	*Lydia takes the apostles into her home*

Prayer Activity

What is most precious to you about the place you call home? Pray for those who have no homes and for those agencies who work to help the homeless. Pray for those who exist in the guarded wealth they call their homes.

Prayer for the Church

Those who bring care and encouragement to people in any kind of need and who work for a healthier society in which all may find fulfilment

especially the Social Care Council, CrossReach, and the staff of the various units it operates.

Blessing

Bless my house O Lord.
Surprise me with strangers,
Surround me with friends,
Give me a door that opens freely
and a table always set.
Build my home as a labour of love.   AMEN

GARDENS

... delight in the gardens ...
~ Song of Solomon 6:2 (Revised English Bible) ~

Senses stimulated;
sights to delight in and dream about.
Sensual and evocative
or more earthy ...
smells,
that bind us with creation.
Textures and tastes,
both familiar and rediscovered.
Birdsong echoing our inner response
to a walk or seat in a garden.

God desires us to enjoy
the beauty of creation;
in our backyards,
allotments and window boxes,
parks and roadsides,
wild and tended.

Yet, there is:
soil to be turned over,
manure to be dug in,
and seeds to be sown.
Flowers need watering and grass cutting,
hedges trimming and trees pruning.
A garden needs planting, tending and love.
A gift to be worked with
as well as enjoyed.
A living thing to invest in
as well as to treasure.

God, thank you for gardens,
small and large,
local and global,
ours and yours.

May we delight in them,
respect them,
enjoy sharing them
and their fruit,
with neighbours and creatures,
great and small.

Readings

Genesis 2:15 *Stewardship*
Jeremiah 29:4–7, 28 *Planting gardens – placemaking and belonging*

Prayer Activity

Buy some fairly traded fruit (fresh or dried) or flowers. As you taste a piece or enjoy the colours, texture or smell, reflect on how we are able to partake of the fruits of our global garden. Give thanks to God for the pleasure and sustenance gardens give us, near and far. Pray for those who grew the products you are enjoying and for others who do not receive a fair price for that which they grow and harvest.

Prayer for the Church

Those who monitor developments in human knowledge and bring the insights of the Gospel to bear so that new discoveries might be used wisely

especially the Society, Religion and Technology Project and the Eco-congregation Project.

Blessing

In our seeing – wonder
In our cultivating – respect
In our trading – justice
In our eating – pleasure.

WORK

The word that came to Jeremiah from the Lord:
'Come, go down to the potter's house, and there I will let you hear my words.'
So I went down to the potter's house, and there he was working at his wheel.

~ Jeremiah 18:1–3 ~

I like to think of that potter, Lord, totally absorbed,
lovingly shaping his creations,
until they are just right for his purpose.
Did he know what use he was to you?
Bless all the potters of this world – in the right place,
just getting on with things,
being faithful in instinctive ways.

Transforming God.
You break into our work.
You startle shepherds minding their own business by night.
You net fishermen and tax collectors upsetting the balance.
You say,
'Come out of the kitchen for a while Martha,
let me feed you.'
You set the jailor free as, finding faith, he cries
'What must I do to be saved?'

Break into my work Lord.
Startle me. Upset the balance in your favour.
Take me out of my comfort zone.
Free me to be and not just to do.
Ready me to go where you call me.

Whatever workplace I am in,
help me to be faithful:
in the way I relate to others,
in the values that my words and actions portray,
in my care of the environment.
I do not want to lead a double life.
It's easier to be faithful among the faithful.

For in my work Lord, paid and unpaid,
I am the unfinished product of your work.
And if others cannot see your hand in me,
I pray, Painstaking Potter,
help me to shape up.
Let me serve your purpose.

Readings

Psalm 92:1–9   *Praise God for the work of his hands*
Jeremiah 18:1–11   *We are the work of God*
Mark 1:16–20 and 2:13–14   *Jesus recruits in the workplaces*
Luke 2:8–20   *An angel appears to the shepherds*
Acts 16:16–34   *The jailer of Paul and Silas is converted*

Prayer Activity

Take a bit of playdough or plasticine. Mould it into the shape of the vessel you think you are. Are we a different shape at different stages of our life? Can we contain more or less sometimes? Trust God to lovingly make you as you need to be at this moment. Be glad that God takes so much care in his work.

Prayer for the Church

Its mission partners working with churches overseas and sharing their concerns (see page 74) and those who work in this country to support church and people in other countries and to remove crippling debt

especially the HIV/AIDS Project, Jubilee Scotland and aid agencies.

Blessing

Bless the places we work O Lord.
Bless the kitchen, the office, the factory,
the school, the supermarket ...
Bless the industrial estates, the shopping centres,
the local communities ...
Bless the whole world,
and Lord, in some small way,
may I be a blessing to it.   AMEN

REST

God rested on the seventh day.
~ Genesis 2:2 (Revised Standard Version) ~

God,
I'm wabbit,[1] I'm weary, I'm worn out.
Often it feels as if I'm running on half empty.
Harassed because it seems I've never enough time to do everything.
Frustrated with my lack of energy to do things as well as I'd like,
or within the timescales I, or others, have set.

Meltdown and breakdown,
exasperation and exhaustion,
sometimes feel just one more step, one more task, away.
And yet,
I know, God, you want it otherwise
for me, for my neighbours, for our world.
When I pause to listen to my body, to nature,
to you,
there is a rhythm which jolts us from frenetic
twenty-first-century living.
A rhythm where rest and relaxation,
fallow periods and holidays are built in.
Not add-ons or extras to be earned.

Forgive me God,
when I abuse your creation –
pushing myself and others too hard.
Help me to follow Jesus' example,
to learn to do nothing regularly,
to practise the art of resting mind, body and spirit.
For you love each one of us for what we are,
and not for what we strive to do.

---

[1] A Scots word meaning tired out.

Readings

Exodus 23:10–12   *Rhythms for the land and human living*

Mark 6:31   *Jesus invites his friends to rest with him*

Prayer Activity

Put a date and time in your diary to take some time for yourself to do nothing but be in a place you find relaxing by yourself.

Prayer for the Church

Those involved in Christian counselling and healing

especially the Christian Fellowship of Healing and other similar groups, and any local group in your church or area.

Blessing

Be still and know that I am God.

Psalm 46:10

NOISE

Make a joyful noise to the Lord, all the earth;
break forth into joyous song and sing praises.
With trumpets and the sound of the horn
make a joyful noise before the King, the Lord.

~ Psalm 98:4–6 ~

Babel, babble, babble, Babel – it makes me laugh, Lord,
This lipsmacking play of plosives.
Babble, Babel, babble, Babel – the one derives from the other,
I know that; and I could look up the meaning
Of 'Babel' in a dusty concordance;
But I'd rather giggle ...

Noise *disorganizes* sound; its excess energy bursts
The wave-forms that doucely carry pitch and timbre.
Its sheer abandon sheerly overwhelms.
That's surely why children love it
And grownups *say* they don't ...

After all, '*a noise*' is just a sound I didn't expect.
Noise is *sounds*, madly polyvocal, chaotically unexpectable.
Uncontrolled – yet also strangely uncontrolling – and so challenging, and liberating
And duly stigmatized ... 'What's all that *noise* ...?'

Is that what you had in mind to teach us,
When you scrambled the organizing sound,
The serried harmonics of command and obedience,
that reduced your lively world to our One Single Human Project?
When you turned the proud sound of human speech
into yet another din – to *noise?*

We speak, Lord, of 'noise *pollution*';
But the noise that pollutes is the noise *we* make, not the noises of creation.
It's the sound of our own voices, our chaotic self-assertion,
Mixed by our pride into a babble, Babel, babble, Babel ...

Is that a sign of your presence, Lord?
Thank God that our cities are babbling Babels
Where life, with its joyous noise is not orchestrated to Our Plan ...

Readings

Genesis 11:1–9   *The tower of Babel*
Joshua 6:1–20   *The walls of Jericho fall*
Psalm 100   *Make a joyful noise to the Lord*
Mark 10:46–52   *Blind Bartimaeus shouts out to Jesus*
Acts 2:1–13   *The day of Pentecost*

Prayer Activity

Don't pick your moment for this. Just do it whenever the thought falls into your head.

Don't find a quiet place.

Don't be by yourself.

Don't close your eyes.

Don't turn off the usual distractions (television, radio, etc.)

Don't necessarily even stay in the house.

Pray anyway. Find God among the babble. And know that you are heard.

Prayer for the Church

As it seeks to develop its spiritual life and become more aware of the God who is in all things and who is with us in our daily life

especially those developing prayer networks and new initiatives in the support of community spiritual life.

Blessing

May the God of life-with-its-bustle-and-noise
Teach us to silence our own imperious voices,
And may we, rather than complaining
That we cannot be heard across the din of life,
Learn to listen in humility for his voice in the babble.

ARTIFICIAL

For he looked forward to the city that has foundations, whose architect and builder is God.

~ Hebrews 11:10 ~

At the genesis of all things, when your Word had been spoken,
When, six times, evening had been, and morning had been,
You looked over all you had made, and it was good. And yet ...

Your work of creation was unfinished, your world not complete, for you,
Until it was lived in.

You offered us your created world to do with what we might
In accordance with our calling as stewards of creation.

We look about us, at what we have made – is it good?

Our built world! Is it possible ...?
Could our hard, brash, burnished surfaces
Our dead-straight horizons, our sky-scraping perpendiculars, our sweeping curves
Our glass stronger than steel, our plastics more durable than rock,
Actually reflect, embody, more than our own glory, pride and hardness?
In our built world, can we actually glorify the Creator
Or do we merely compete and defy?

In our built world – can we commune with you?

We offer you our built world, to do with as you will
In accordance with your being as gracious, loving God.

Complete in us your work of redemption: help *us* to complete *our* world
By building in it good lives to your glory.

When evening comes, and when morning comes
Give us to look at all that we have made, and call down God's blessing
On the cities, villages and habitations of our built world.

Readings

Genesis 1:1 — 2:3   *God creates the heavens and the earth*
1 Kings 8:12–30   *Solomon prays to God to dwell in his temple*
Nehemiah 2:1–8   *Nehemiah asks to return to rebuild Jerusalem*
Psalm 122   *In praise of Jerusalem*
Matthew 7:24–9   *The wise and foolish builders*

Prayer Activity

Somewhere in your house, you will have an 'image library'. *You* might call it a photo album, or a glossy magazine, or 'that tin where I keep all the postcards'! Or you could go online … Whatever, flick through some images, pictures of the real world. Find something man-made that appeals to you, that lifts your soul. Why does it lift your soul? What in it reflects the creativity, the accommodating grace, even the *hospitality* – or indeed any other aspect – of God?

Prayer for the Church

Those who are concerned that the physical surroundings of the local church assist towards deeper worship, warmer hospitality and stronger witness

especially the Committee on Church Art and Architecture.

Blessing

May God,
Whom heaven and highest heaven cannot contain,
Much less the houses we build,
Be nevertheless the God
In whom we live, and move, and have our being,
As we build our lives in our built world,
That the work of our hands
May be to his glory.

TREES

Praise the Lord from the earth you ... fruit trees and all cedars.
~ Psalm 148:7, 9 ~

Oh give thanks to the Lord for the glory of trees!

Urban trees, rural trees, highway trees, public open space trees,
woodlands, hedgerows and orchards,
ancient trees and newly planted trees.

Oh give thanks to the Lord for the glory of trees!

Trees that generate oxygen and store carbon,
that play host to a spectacular variety of wildlife,
and provide us with raw materials and shelter.

Oh give thanks to the Lord for the glory of trees!

Trees bring better health, make more attractive landscapes,
Provide less pollution, soil stabilization
and flood alleviation.

Oh give thanks to the Lord for the glory of trees!

Trees offer us respite and inspire our imaginations,
Provide creativity and culture,
Restore and refresh our souls.

Oh give thanks to the Lord for the glory of trees!

Trees under threat
with ecosystems fragmented and disturbed,
hacked down to make way for houses, motorways and airports.

A world without trees would be barren, impoverished and intolerable.

So give thanks to the Lord for the glory of trees!

Readings

Genesis 2:9 — 3:24	*Producing good fruit*
Genesis 13:18, 14:13, 18:1	*Sacred trees*
Judges 9:7–21	*Trees together*
Psalm 104	*Creation praise*
Matthew 7:15–20	*A fruit tree*
Mark 11:12–2	*Palm trees*

Prayer Activity

Trees absorb carbon dioxide (a principle contributor to global warming) from the atmosphere and store it, while releasing oxygen back out. If we are going to help with global warming, we need to plant more trees! So ... save up some money to plant a tree! Tress can be given as gifts for birthdays, weddings, celebrations. Be in contact with your local forestry commission or look up these websites:

www.Plant-A-Tree-Today.org

www.treesforlife.org.uk

www.treeforall.org.uk

Prayer for the Church

Those who are in my own congregation, helping it to be part of the living, witnessing Church

especially those who challenge me and my brothers and sisters into fresh new adventures of witness and mission.

Blessing

May tree and hill, rock and river
reflect your glory, God.
May all your creation rest in harmony
At the end of the day
to know your peace.   AMEN

Sky

I love the pictures that children paint of landscapes. The ones where there is great green-brown land at the bottom of the page and bright blue sky right at the top and then a great expanse of white paper left in the middle. Perhaps this articulates something about our sense that sky is 'out there', 'up there', somehow disconnected from us, above us and beyond us. It may also articulate our sense of God – still 'up there' (on a cloud), 'above us' and 'beyond us'. Sky seems to sum up the enormity of God – the vastness and hugeness of the universe – too much to take in. It is the place where we look up in awe and marvel at that which is beyond our understanding and control.

Sky is the environment of mystery. It is full of myth, magic and wonder.

STARS

*It is I, Jesus, who sent my angel to you with this testimony for the churches.
I am the root and the descendant of David, the bright morning star.*

~ Revelation 22:16 ~

O Little Star
Twinkling in the darkness
Bringing out the child in us
full of awe and wonder at the vastness of the universe
and the mysterious unknown, yet to be discovered.

O North Star
Guiding the traveller
Holding steadfast with a bright beam to point the way
And guide us in the right direction.

O Lost Star
Hiding behind light pollution
Living out our need for more heat and light
Has taken its toll on the sustainability of the earth.

O Morning Star
Revealing Christ in the dawn
Fallen from heaven to dwell amongst us on earth.

O God who created the stars
Be for us a light
Fill us with excitement at the wonder of the universe
Guide us as we seek out a path and a direction
Be present with us even when we strain to see your light.

Be for us a star
Bright, shining, twinkling, guiding, revealing –
A star that breaks through the dawn
A presence for the day.

Readings

Isaiah 14:12	*Israel is like a fallen star*
Matthew 2:2–10	*The wise men follow the star*
1 Corinthians 15:41	*The glory of the stars*
2 Peter 1:19	*The morning star will rise in your hearts*
Revelation 2:28	*To the one who conquers I will give the morning star*

Prayer Activity

It may be difficult to see stars if you live in an urban context where light pollution prevents us from seeing them clearly. However, if you can, try to gaze up at the stars and just marvel at the vastness of them! Perhaps you could learn a pattern of one of the constellations and then try to spot it in the sky at different times of the year.

Prayer for the Church

Centres to which people may withdraw to renew body and mind and to engage more deeply in worship and study, seeking the relevance of the Gospel for the modern world

especially all retreat centres and places of calm and quiet in a busy world, providing rest and recreation of the spirit.

Blessing

Holy One
Be a bright light in our fear of the darkness
Be a guiding light when we have lost our way
Be a starlight radiant in the universe
Shining out your light on all the earth.

RAINBOW

I have set my bow in the clouds and it shall be a sign of the covenant between me and the earth.

~ Genesis 9:13 ~

Projected through the moist air
on to the cloudy canvas
the sun breaks through!
An arc of glorious colours
transforming the environment
and reflecting the promise of God.
God, the Maker
who calls humanity into a Rainbow Coalition.

Lord,
I hear that term so often in the news
to describe some uneasy alliance
between different political or social groups
each pursuing their own agenda.
That's not what you meant, is it?

Imagine all the people
living life as you intended!
The full spectrum of the human race
united in common promise
to nourish one another,
to cherish the earth,
to revere your world.

Is this just a childlike dream?

Lord,
I don't want to grow out of it.
I love rainbows.
They fill me with hope and joy
and belief in the goodness of life.
I don't want my reality reduced to black and/or white.

Help me to keep striving for colours –
until the day the rainbow
dwells upon the earth.

Readings

Genesis 9:8–17	*God's covenant with Abraham*
Ezekiel 1:1–28	*The splendour of the glory of God is like a rainbow*
Revelation 4:1–11	*A rainbow around the heavenly throne*
Revelation 10:1–11	*The angel with a rainbow over his head*

Prayer Activity

The rainbow was God's sign of love and healing. In your mind, picture a rainbow and bask in its glory. Now try to *hear* a rainbow. What would it sound like? An African father of fourteen children said, 'We can't all speak at once in the family but we can all sing!'

Prayer for the Church

The increasing number of people who choose to relate to the Church less through traditional membership patterns and more through general commitment and particular projects

especially Christian Aid and all agencies concerned with the homeless and healing of God's people.

Blessing

May God bless your dreams,
and may your dream and his
become one. AMEN

ECLIPSE

From noon on, darkness came over the whole land until three in the afternoon.
And about three o'clock, Jesus cried with a loud voice, 'Eli, Eli, lema
sabachthani?' that is, 'My God, my God, why have you forsaken me?'

~ Matthew 27:45–6 ~

Jesus,
human suffering Jesus,
in that cry of desolation
you opened your arms to everyone
who has been visited
by the darkness of overwhelming absence.
In the anguish of feeling alone, forsaken,
betrayed even,
we too cry out:
'Where are you, God?
If, you really exist
how can you let this happen?'

Yet Jesus, like you, we are still in conversation:
daring to expect a response, trusting that the shadow will pass,
clinging to the promise that you are with us always.

Thank you for making it OK to tell God just how it feels!
Friends try to help, telling us
that it is we, not God, who have turned away.
Even if there is truth in that.
We feel abandoned.
For when we feel blocked from your light O God,
how do we know which way to turn?
Are you asking us to embrace the darkness?

Jesus gives us permission.
We too can be honest –
with ourselves, with others, with you, God.

Ever present, all seeing Lord,
nothing in heaven or on earth can eclipse us from your sight.
Wherever we are, you are.

Whatever happens you can lead us on from there.
Lord, Jesus Christ, Saviour,
thank God for your eclipse,
else, none of us could move on.

Readings

Psalm 139:1–18	*The inescapable God*
Amos 8:1–12	*Vision of the basket of fruit*
Micah 3:1–8	*False prophets in the shadows*
Matthew 27:45–55	*Jesus on the cross*
1 Corinthians 13:1–13	*For now we see through a mirror dimly*

Prayer Activity

On a winter's night when you go to bed, you switch out the light. At first the room is dark, full of the unknown. You let yourself be enfolded by the darkness. Then little by little, the darkness lightens. A faintly discernible source of light brings misty outlines of familiar shapes. Thank God for the light. Pray for those in an eclipse.

Prayer for the Church

My own part in the Church and the special gifts I have given which, in unity with others, build up the body of Christ

especially the forgotten skill and abilities, those which may lead me into new and exciting adventures of faith.

Blessing

'If I say, "Surely the darkness shall cover me
and the light around me become night."
even the darkness is not dark to you;
the night is as bright as the day,
for darkness is as light to you.'

Psalm 139:11–12

Lord lead me on to be a light for others.
Lead me on till the break of day.   AMEN

LIGHTNING

Now as [Saul] was going along and approaching Damascus, suddenly a light from heaven flashed around him.

~ Acts 9:3 ~

The opera of nature!
Percussion of thunder and hail,
as the Creator's strobe lighting flashes through the cloud-laden sky.
The air is charged with the presence of God.

Do we run? Do we hide?
Do we fall on our knees and bow our heads?
Or do we watch and wonder in sheer humility
at the glory and majesty of God?

When the sounds effects cease,
and the pyrotechnics are over,
things will not be the same as before.
Dazzled by the unexpected, Saul met God,
and, in so doing, met himself.
Dulled by the expected and the accepted,
we lose our edge and vision,
until a flash of revelation hits the mark
and we remember who we are.

Lightning strikes at the heart of humanity:
God's and ours.
The flashes of gunfire that pierce the sky,
the clouds of the bombs that blast a village.
The air is charged with hatred and terror.
When the sound effects cease and the pyrotechnics are over,
things will not be the same as before.
There will be devastation.
There will be death.
There will be the cries of the wounded and the bereaved.
How long O God, how long?

Blind those who can see only violence and bloodshed
as the means to justice.

Bless those who are persecuted unjustly.
Be with families and communities torn apart by war.

Baptize us with your lightning,
remind us of our identity.
Empower us to be justice seekers and peacemakers
who are marked by the Light.

Readings

Exodus 9:22–9 *God's lightning, thunder and hail*
2 Samuel 22:1–20 *David's song of thanksgiving*
Matthew 28:1–9 *The angel's appearance was like lightning*
Acts 9:1–9 *Saul's conversion*

Prayer Activity

In 'Watching for the Kingfisher', the poet Ann Lewin describes prayer as like watching for a kingfisher. You wait in what you think is the right place trusting that you will be given a visible sign of his presence. Then when you have almost stopped expecting anything, *'a flash of brightness gives encouragement'*. To what extent is this your own experience? What have been the 'aha' moments in your life? Now focus outwards. Pray for 'aha' moments for those whose actions bring darkness to others.

Prayer for the Church

Those who ensure that the fabric of church buildings is maintained and that the Church's heritage in buildings is conserved for the good of the Church and the nation

especially the General Trustees.

Blessing

May you see and hear the signs of God:
in nature,
in the environment,
in others,
in yourself.
And may the love of the Creator,
the Mediator Christ,
and the Transforming Spirit
live in you now and forevermore. AMEN

HORIZON

*I was there when he set the heavens in place
When he marked out the horizon on the face of the deep.*
~ Proverbs 8:27 (New International Version) ~

Horizon
The moment when earth and heaven meet
Watching the setting sun, waiting until the last ray disappears from view
It's often achingly hard to let go, to acknowledge endings.

Horizon
The moment when earth and heaven meet
Shrouded in mystery as the mist settles in the distance
We cannot see through the haze and the way ahead is unclear.

Horizon
The moment when earth and heaven meet
Carrying the expectation of the traveller longing for the 'more' of life
Seeking and searching for meaning and purpose.

Horizon
The moment when earth and heaven meet
The sun sets on our day to be greeted by someone else's dawn
Full of hope and fresh beginnings.

Horizon
The moment when earth and heaven meet
We glimpse
You God who comes to us in this revelation
That we can be more
That we are called beyond the boundary of our belief
To a new relationship with you.

Readings

Luke 17:24   *The Son of Man will light up the sky*
Job 26:10   *God defines the boundaries*
Nehemiah 1:9   *The people return from the farthest points*

Prayer Activity

Spend time looking at the horizon – what do you notice? What do you see? What does it mean for you? How might looking at the horizon help you to pray?

Prayer for the Church

Those engaged in new, creative ministries and those who faithfully and energetically serve the parishes of our Lord.

Blessing

Bless to us our dreams and our longings
Bless to us the moments we gaze into the distance
Seeking and searching for the more of life
Bless to us the places where heaven and earth meet
In the horizons of our lives.

CLOUDS

And the glory of the Lord appeared in the cloud.

~ Exodus 16:10 ~

God of mystery,
near at hand yet beyond ...

The clouds in the sky
at times mirror my moods
and my situation.

Grey and flat and boring,
black, foreboding and potentially thunderous.
Or, light and whispy,
dancing across the sky.
All of life reflected in the clouds.

Blocks to the radiant Sun,
surrounding hilltops,
enveloping aeroplanes ...
preventing us seeing all.
Yet evoking mystery –
what is beyond our sight?

Clouds –
beckoning my imagination
to see shapes and faces and features
to lie back and watch and dream.
Clouds –
blown across the sky
by a force beyond their control.

Help me to be energized
by another wind
which seeks to direct my journey
if I too am responsive.

Readings

Exodus 13:17–22   *A pillar of cloud to guide*
Exodus 40:33–8   *Mystery, otherness and clouds*

Prayer Activity

Take time to sit or lie and look at the clouds. Focus on them – their shapes, their movement, their texture. What do you see? What do you imagine? What may be beyond?

Prayer for the Church

Those who ensure that the local church is well supported and staffed and who take initiatives in mission and outreach where people live, work and take leisure

especially the Priority Areas Fund, and chaplaincies in hospitals, education, industry, prisons and residential homes.

Blessing

Gentle breeze,
Blowing wind,
Buffeting gale.
Holy spirit
direct my journey,
not across the skies
but through each day of my life.

Alienating

We all find ourselves, at some time, in alienating places. Perhaps we drift there unaware, maybe others place us there, or we may even make a deliberate choice to withdraw.

Alienating landscapes – physical and spiritual – can be desperately lonely and isolated, even when they are crowded. Yet there is also a strange comfort to be had in being not a part, but apart.

God himself knows alienation. He wandered in deserts, walked among outcasts, endured rejection and felt the harshness of betrayal. Perhaps that is why he understands so well when we feel different and distant. Perhaps that is why, even at what seems our most unreachable, he reaches to touch us.

Prayer, in the midst of alienation, can be a challenge. Words become as inaccessible and lifeless as the place in which we wander. Yet it is often in the most remote, estranged and distant spaces of our surroundings and souls that we hear God's voice most clearly. It may be only a whisper from the depths of our despair, a sense of something in the nothing, a defiant cry above the noise or a glimmer of light in the gloom but still it comes, clear and loud and persistent.

God enters the very heart of who and where we are, drawing us from exile into intimacy with him, and community with one another.

BARRENNESS

*I am the vine, you are the branches. Those who abide in me and I in them
bear much fruit, because apart from me you can do nothing.*

~ John 15:5 ~

There is expectation in nothingness;
an opening waiting to be filled.
An opportunity to make of it what you will.

Lord, it's been hard to grow this past while.
I've spread out my branches
only for them to scrape and score and wither.
My fruit has been a little too bitter
and hard to swallow at times.
And I've yearned for nourishment
in the barren places of my parched soul.

There is expectation in nothingness;
an opening waiting to be filled.
an opportunity to make of it what you will.

I have been here before, Lord,
and I am reluctant to explore again
the emptiness that aches and echoes.
So remind me, as I scan for signs of life,
that in the wasteland
an old man dreams,
a woman laughs,
a baby cries,
flowers grow a pathway for the poor
and God says it is good.

There is expectation in nothingness;
an opening waiting to be filled.
An opportunity to make of it what you will.

Make of me what you will, Lord.
Take what little life there is and make it good.   AMEN

Readings

Genesis 18:1–15 *Abraham and Sarah*
Psalm 46:8–11 *Be still, and know that I am God*
Mark 11:12–14 *Jesus curses the fig tree*

Prayer Activity

Take a blank sheet of paper and draw a circle on it. Write inside the circle the aspects of your life that are comfortable and productive. Now write outside the circle those aspects you feel are dry and unfruitful. Pray about how you might bring those aspects inside the circle.

Prayer for the Church

As it meets in local Church councils where support is given and policies made

especially the Presbyteries, their Moderators and Clerks; Kirk Sessions and Session Clerks; Congregational Boards, Committees of Management, Deacons' Courts and their Clerks.

Blessing

May God's living entwine you
His life fill you
and his love bear fruit
in you and those you meet.
And may you know fulfilment
in the freshness
and the fullness
of the life-giving Christ
today and always.   AMEN

MIST/FOG

For he draws up the drops of water, he distils his mist in rain.

~ Job 36:27 ~

Remind us, Lord, how blindness can see what is there,
While sight can for a while be blinded.

(There is a story
Of an old man, devout and humble
Brought back for a day to the valley where he had spent his youth.

The courtesy car stopped, high on the pass,
And he was got out, and shown the view he knew so well.
His eyes moved over it, and he muttered audibly
'Well done, God!'

That radiant evening, going home,
He stopped his lift again in that place.
The valley was full of mist; the view, as such, had gone;
Why stop at all?
His eyes ranged over what he knew was there
And he could say once more, 'Well done, God!'
Because he was blind, and didn't need to see. He knew.)

Lord, we panic when we cannot see,
When the mist begins to rise, and sight to dim,
Or when the whelming fog enfolds,
Whitening out our sight – our sharpened senses mocked
Because we can place nothing.

Then we can either *know*,
Or allow ourselves to be led by those who know.
Either demands trust – trust that you are there
Or at any rate trust in lives lived in that trust.

Remind us that we are only really in a fog, Lord
When what we see prevents us from seeing;
Or when not seeing prevents us from trusting.

Readings

2 Kings 6:8–23	*The Arameans are struck blind*
Mark 8:23–38	*Jesus heals a blind man* (several different kinds of fog in this complex passage!)
Mark 10:46–52	*Blind Bartimaeus*
1 Corinthians 13, especially verse 12	*Now we see in a mirror dimly*
Hebrews 11:1ff.	*The conviction of things not seen* (try several translations, if you have them to hand)

Prayer Activity

Close your eyes! No – *don't* pray, just close your eyes, and ask yourself 'What just happened?' Or blindfold yourself. Just that. Sit and reflect on what is coming in, not just from other senses, but from the sense of sight. Ask – don't try to formulate answers.

And if you are blind or partially sighted, please forgive the inevitable crudities of this groping for meaning. What arises for you from your sighted friends' attempts to grope with this whole area? What could you tell us, in the fog in which we grope? What could you tell us of God-where-you-are?

Prayer for the Church

As it explores and renews its faith in the contemporary context and lifts the world and its people to God in praise and prayer

especially the Scottish Storytelling Centre and the wider work of the Netherbow.

Blessing

God be our vision;
God be our security when we cannot see;
God be our trust when we are not sure;
God be our courage when we do not understand;
Christ be our vision of God.

LONELY PLACE

Look on my right hand and see –
there is no one who takes notice of me;
no refuge remains to me;
no one cares to me.

~ Psalm 142:4 ~

Sometimes,
I go to that place called Lonely
I go there by myself or with companions
and stay a long while or just for a short time.
It's a place that aches with abandonment
A place where even the tears have run dry.
And I long to know God
Will I ever find you there?

No one talks about visiting this place
It carries a stigma
hidden in many disguises.

The child in the playground that no one plays with
The awkward teenager – too big, too small, too fat, too tall
The clubber dancing wildly fearing the day's end
The person with learning disabilities that has never known a friend
The single person left out by couples who dine
The parent longing for adult conversation
The widow/er grieving a companionship of love
The old person at home or in a home, wondering if this is
all that's to show for life well lived.

Sometimes,
I go to that place called Lonely
A place where I
Long to seek you God.
Where I ache
for
Someone.
Some.
One.

Readings

Psalms 42, 63	*My soul thirsts for God*
Psalms 69, 77, 102, 130	*Out of the depths I cry to you, O Lord*
Matthew 26:36–46	*Jesus in Gethsemane*

Prayer Activity

Think about the difference between being lonely and being alone. Loneliness is a disease that is sweeping our world and we rarely talk about it. Think of someone who may be feeling lonely – pray for them and try and do something to let them know they are not alone.

Prayer for the Church

Those who guide and administer the details of the Church's life at national level

especially the Central Services Committee, and all who look after the welfare of pensioners and the retired.

Blessing

God, when we most need it
Come close to us who are lonely,
with the voice of a stranger
the care of a neighbour
the smile of a child
the conversation of a friend.
God, when we most need it
Do not forget us who are lonely.

VOID

But he himself went a day's journey into the wilderness, and came and sat down under a broom tree; and he asked that he might die, saying, 'It is enough; now, O LORD, take away my life; for I am no better than my fathers.'

~ 1 Kings 19:4 (Revised Standard Version) ~

It is as though creation were undone.
I open my eyes and see
all that I saw before;
but its substance – I realize – has drained away.
When did this happen? How many days have I been like this?

The colours of existence are no less vivid
but something has drained out of them;
What I touch and see feel and seem as solid
as ever they did – yet insubstantial.
Life is suddenly a drudge's performance,
The warmth of people a facsimile,
Loving smiles mere facial contortions.
'*All that is solid melts into air.*'

It is as though the whole of reality
were a thin skin, stretched over nothing;
Over the void …
If I were to scratch it with my fingernail, it would flake away,
Revealing … maybe *nothing* …

But what would nothing look like?
Maybe just like this.

I am terrified of the void, Lord – when it does not make me numb.
It's so easy, when it *doesn't* confront me,
To say resonantly 'Well, of course, God fills the void – because he is God!'
Which is true, of course. But how far does it take me?
For when this emptiness faces me, I need to be able to say
'God filled the void by emptying himself –
By becoming what *I am* …'

And I can. Teach me how …

Readings

Genesis 1	*The earth was a formless void*
Psalm 22	*My God, why have you forsaken me?*
Mark 15:33–9	*Darkness at the crucifixion*
Philippians 2:1–11	*Christ emptied himself*
Hebrews 2:10–18	*Jesus made perfect by suffering*

Prayer Activity

Martin Luther suffered all his life from the most crushing depression. When everything else seemed to him to have been evacuated of meaning, when the void seemed to whelm up and threaten to swallow him, he would take a piece of chalk and write on the table 'I have been baptized' ('Baptizatus sum' in Latin). That, for him, was something ineradicably of God. He could cling to that. Think about this in the context of prayer. What thoughts spring from it, for you?

Prayer for the Church

Those who witness to the living Christ in the midst of his people, in Word and Sacrament, those who as deacons lead the Church in living out the Gospel, and those who recruit, train and support them.

especially the Ministries Council.

Blessing

Of the Fullness of Being he emptied himself out.
For us and with us – and also before us
He came into the void, and allowed the void into him.
Crying out his dereliction, he overcame.
So he who is Way, Truth and Life
Will always be our road
From the Void back to the Fullness of Being.

CROWDED

The crowds that went ahead of him and that followed were shouting 'Hosanna to the Son of David! Blessed is the one who comes in the name of the Lord!'

~ Matthew 21:9 ~

Right in the midst, making a way where no way appeared –
Jesus, you came into the crowded street.
To euphoric cheers and excited waves,
You rode into town and the crowd went wild!

God, we know that you are community,
And there is something in us that seeks togetherness:
Harmony in music, chanting in numbers,
Clapping, waving, surging – one body, one movement.

But God we remember today,
those who feel lonely even in the busiest street,
those who have stopped listening in the noisiest party,
those who can't cope with surround sound
who feel claustrophobic with people all around.

God of the festival –
May your energy move us to shout and sing,
Dance and stretch
But far from the crowd in our own space
May we know our own minds
And know that you, still, are God.

Readings

Matthew 21:1–11   *Palm Sunday*
Matthew 26:36–46   *Gethsemane*

Prayer Activity

Imagine being in the Palm Sunday crowd. What sounds do you hear, what colours and sights do you see, how are you physically moved, how do you feel? Now move to Gethsemane – now what sounds, what sights, what feelings do you have? Share these places and experiences with God.

Prayer for the Church

The Church as it takes shape in areas where there are special difficulties – social, economic or health-related

especially the Mission and Discipleship Council in its work in mission and evangelism, worship, doctrine, education and nurture.

Blessing

Just as I am, though tossed about
With many a conflict, many a doubt,
Fightings and fears within, without,
O Lamb of God, I come.

DEPTHS

The Kingdom of God is within us.
~ Luke 17:21 (Good News Bible) ~

God,
the depths of your creation contain resources
on which we depend –
for energy, for sustenance,
for survival.

In the depths of the oceans,
towards the core of the earth,
we trawl,
we excavate,
we drill …
to find untapped sources
of oil, food and water.

Help us,
to dare to explore
the depths of our inner being
to discover or rediscover anew,
resources which may enhance our lives,
the lives of others
and our relationship with you.

Inner murmurings and voices,
yearnings and stirrings,
dreams and visions
which speak of you,
point to you
and the coming of your Kingdom of Peace and Justice.

Readings

Psalm 78:15–16   *Physical resources from the depths of the earth to be shared*

Luke 17:20–1   *Spiritual resources from inner depths to be shared and brought into being*

Prayer Activity

Keep a note of your dreams (both day-dreams and those you remember from during the night). Ask God to help you understand what they might be telling you. Perhaps chat to someone you trust about them. How may acting on your dreams and aspirations enhance your life and the lives of others?

Prayer for the Church

As it explores and renews its faith in the contemporary context and lifts the world and its people to God in praise and prayer

especially all engaged in leading and planning worship, and those who study and write about what Christians believe.

Blessing

God be in our hearts and in our loving,
God be in our minds and in our thinking,
God be in our gut, and in our feeling,
God be in our dreams and in our discerning,
God be in our depths, your Kingdom revealing.

Elemental

To 'surrender' oneself to or to be 'battered' by the elements are expressions often used by people about to venture outside in all weathers. The weather and its elements are indeed powerful forces and, more and more in our world, we see countries and people overwhelmed by extreme floods and hurricanes, storms and even cyclones.

The Bible often alludes to the presence or voice of God as being in storms. How true it is, that power beyond our comprehension and elements we cannot properly predict or understand, points beyond ourselves to the awesome mystery of the world's creator. The elements we experience day in, day out, rain, hail or shine, although essentially external to our windows and our bodies, have a profound effect on our inner moods and sense of well-being. Could it be that the voice of God, even if still and small, speaks to us here too?

RAIN

They are like clouds carried along by the wind but bringing no rain.

~ Jude 1:12 ~

Battering against the window
Drenching every object
A wall of water outside the door
Barrs the way
and stops us going out.

Rain carried in dark clouds
oppressively hovering
Changing every mood and plan
Brings disappointment and
Dampens our spirits.

Yet, God of the living water,
Today we give thanks for the rain,
For all it refreshes and cleanses and nourishes.

Help us enjoy an opportunity to be indoors
Appreciating all that is within.
Help us to notice growing and greening
In our world around us.
Help us savour the taste of clean water,
Forgive our moaning and groaning at the weather
As we remember those who see dark clouds that bring no rain.

Readings

John 4:1–42   *Living water*
Matthew 5:43–8   *Refreshing attitude*

Prayer Activity

As you shower or bathe this day, every time you use water, remember you are a baptized child of God – every day God pours his goodness and love upon you. How does that knowledge affect how you face this day?

Prayer for the Church

Those who speak for the Church and show the relevance of the Gospel for our life in society

especially the Church and Society Council and the Scottish Churches' Parliamentary Office.

Blessing

It's world of sunshine, a world of rain;
It's a world of laughter, a world of pain;
It's a world we must share, where we must learn to care,
For the world belongs to God.
This is God's world after all,
This is God's world after all,
This is God's world after all,
Yes, it's God's good world.

CH4 245

EBB AND FLOW

Now there was a woman who had been suffering from haemorrhages for twelve years.

~ Mark 5:25 ~

Lifeblood.
Lifeblood ebbing away:
from the fragmenting memory of the confused,
from the haemorrhaging imagination of the mentally ill,
from the anguished mind of those obsessed with deadlines,
from the pierced heart of the loved one left behind.

Lifeblood emptying:
from the hopes of the young man void of all purpose,
from the self-esteem of the girl sucked into the sex trade,
from the back-broken bodies of those slaving for a pittance,
from the tortuous shell of the chronically or acutely ill.

God bless all who bleed.
Jesus show us how to be healers.
Spirit comfort us. More blood donors are needed.
Prayer is not enough.

For touching, actually touching!
Power ebbs away from the body of Christ.
Flows into the one who bleeds!
Sacrifice is not always needed. Offering will do.

Lifeblood.
Lifeblood flowing through:
listening places with the lost, the lonely and the confused,
hands of friendship to the outcast and the terrified,
acts of justice for the abused and the exploited,
an ending to one nation's resources ebbing away in a tide of debt.

Lifeblood flowing from the cross.
Lord, when I drink from the cup,
may I remember why I am here.
Lifeblood.

Readings

Isaiah 2:2–3   *Nations shall flow to the temple of the Lord*
Isaiah 48:17–21   *Blessings flowing*
Job 1:13–22   *The Lord gives and the Lord takes away*
Job 42:10–17   *Job's blessings are restored*
John 7:37–44   *Living water flows from the hearts of believers*

Prayer Activity

Think of the sea. See the waves flowing in and watch the tide ebb back. Does the sea land blessings on the shore? What does the tide draw back into itself? Hear the rhythm in your head. Think of the ebb and flow of your life. Which current is stronger just now? Is there a rhythm? What do you give to others? What do you draw from others?

Prayer for the Church

As it seeks new patterns of ministry and mission for the more effective use of personnel and a stronger interface with the community

especially those in new charge developments and changing patterns and situations ministry.

Blessing

The Lord will keep your going out
and your coming in,
from this time on and forever more.
Thanks be to God.   AMEN

WIND

He said, 'Come.' So Peter got out of the boat, started walking on the water and came towards Jesus. But when he noticed the strong wind he became frightened, and beginning to sink, he cried out, 'Lord, save me!'

~ Matthew 14:29–30 ~

Hear, said the wind,
and I waited, breathless, for a word,
amidst the curling, twisting currents
that spattered sprays of doubt among my certainty.

Come, said the wind,
and just that once
I let it lift and carry me,
gently up and out from the safety of my shelter.

Walk, said the wind,
and as it whipped and played
around my head and feet
I felt its tug towards impossible horizons.

Trust, said the wind
and raised its mighty head
as shameful I looked down
towards the frightful blackness of my fears.

Take, said the wind,
and with just one touch
I was storm-surfing,
borne and buffeted by promises of forever.

Know, said the wind
and went on its way,
leaving whispers in its wake,
and sighs that speak forever in my soul.

Be always in our lives, Lord,
with words of comfort and call,
danger and dreaming,
that we might dare to step closer.

Readings

Exodus 14:21–5   *The parting of the Red Sea*
Matthew 14:22–33   *Jesus calms the storm*
Acts 2:1–4   *The coming of the Holy Spirit*

Prayer Activity

Think of the times God has rushed into your life like a whirlwind, or crept in gently like a breeze. Give thanks for those moments when you were touched by his presence.

Prayer for the Church

Those who bring their creativity to bear on making known the Gospel, in print, film, news media, sound and website

especially Saint Andrew Press, Life & Work, *the Publishing Committee, and those who maintain the Church's website.*

Blessing

God's arms in the solitude
God's hand in the crowd.
God's word in the silence
God's whisper in the noise.
God's voice in the darkness.
God's echo in the light.
God's calm in the conflict
God's rhythm in the harmony.
God's help in the possible
God's hope in the impossible.
God's touch in the breeze
God's kiss in the raindrops.
God's comfort in the Spirit.
God's love in your life.   AMEN

FLOOD

The waters swelled and increased greatly on the earth; and the ark floated on the face of the waters.

~ Genesis 7:18 ~

Rushing gushing flashing crashing creeping sweeping
surging purging flowing growing turning churning.
Here it comes, Lord, with a furious passion,
your all-consuming love.

Tossing jostling whirling swirling pitching ditching
gripping tipping heaving weaving shaking breaking.
Here I am, Lord, head amongst the froth,
faith as my compass.

When I'm dry and stranded, aground among the shingle,
always you come, Lord,
flooding parched plains with songs and second chances.
Then I throw together the wood of my life
praying it carries me
till you hold out branches as a sign that solid ground is near.

Groping hoping beaching reaching reeling feeling
landing standing tested rested embraced with grace.
Here we are, Lord, raised together on rainbows,
ready to begin again.
Amen.

Readings

1 Kings 18:30–9   *Elijah's sacrifice*
Psalms 46:1–7   *God is our refuge*
Psalm 69:1–18   *Save me, O God*
Matthew 7:24–7   *The man who built his house on a rock*

Prayer Activity

Draw a rainbow. Write an aspect of your life to match each colour. Why is it that colour? Would you rather it was another? Pray about how you may change it. Return to your rainbow each day for the next week (seven days/seven colours) and see how it changes.

Prayer for the Church

Those who seek to renew the life and mission of the Church, develop strategies and establish priorities

especially the Council of Assembly, the Panel for Review and Reform, and the Church without Walls Initiative.

Blessing

God of wonder and wave
God of time and torrent
God of surprise and surge,
pour into our lives
the power of your blessing
that we might be
caressed and carried
in the swirling strength
of your grace.
Through Jesus Christ our Lord. AMEN

HURRICANE

You ride on the wings of the wind, you make the winds your messengers, fire and flame your ministers.

~ Psalm 104:3–4 ~

Strong winds blowing,
Trees fallen, branches ripped,
Homes damaged, debris strewn,
People shaken and unsteadied …
When the wild winds blow, God, we feel the power.

Strong winds blowing,
Waves crash on shores,
Children seek shelter,
Outside is dangerous,
Inside hears swirling gusts,
creaking roofs and doors …
When the hurricane comes, God, we feel in its path.

Strong God, powerful force in our lives
When we see the wind's destruction,
When we feel the speed,
When we hear the unyielding storm
What are you saying to us?
For the winds are your messengers,
Fire and flame your ministers,
The world is your creation and we are its stewards.

Strong winds blow, hard lessons are learned,
Complacent lives are shaken,
the flame of the faithful is fanned with new vigour,
You have spoken, help us listen.

Readings

Psalm 104   *God rides on the wings of the wind*
Matthew 24:31   *The gathering of the elect*
Luke 8:22–5   *The storm on the lake*
Hebrews 1:7   *He makes his angels winds*

Prayer Activity

In the midst of a fierce and frightening storm, when a strong wind blew upon the disciples' boat, Jesus calmed the storm and asked them 'Where is your faith?' When have you experienced a storm in your life? Where was your faith?

Prayer for the Church

Those who offer special expertise to local congregations as they seek to develop their work, worship and witness

especially the Regional Development Officers of the Mission and Discipleship Council.

Blessing

Will your anchor hold in the straits of fear,
When the breakers roar and the reef is near?
While the surges rave and the wild winds blow,
Shall the angry waves then your bark o'erflow?

FIRE

The Lord went in front of them in a pillar of cloud by day, to lead them along the way, and in a pillar of fire by night, to give them light, so they might travel by day and by night.

~ Exodus 13:21 ~

It will burn, child.
Swift and sharp
as the slice of shimmering steel.

It will burn, child.
Scorching and shocking
as words spat in heated haste.

It will burn, child.
Stinging and scabbing
as fresh scars smart with rage.

And so we learn, Lord, to fear the fire
should it hurt and harm us;
damage and deny us;
wound and waste us.

Then you come, guiding God,
shimmering and flickering and shouting
Yes, child, it will burn, but see me.
Yes, child, it will burn, but follow me.
Yes, child, it will burn, but it is for you.

Bring me bare foot, Lord,
to feel your heat sear and seal my soul.
Lead me with a love that crackles with life,
that demands and dances;
pains and purifies;
brings newness from the scorched earth
of my lukewarm life.

It will burn, Lord.
But I am ready.

Readings

Exodus 3:2   *Moses and the burning bush*
Isaiah 6:1–8   *Isaiah's calling*
Matthew 3:11–12   *He will baptize you with fire*
Acts 2:1–4   *The coming of the Holy Spirit*

Prayer Activity

Light a candle and watch the flame. Concentrate on the different colours, shapes and shadows it casts. Think of the areas of your life that need purified, speak each one into the flame and pray for them to be refined.

Prayer for the Church

Those who guide the Church in temporal matters and see that, in its dealings, justice prevails

especially the Law Department and the Safeguarding Unit.

Blessing

Come, Lord
with flaming fearlessness,
Come, Lord,
with blazing boldness.
Come, Lord,
to burnish and bless
lives dulled,
hopes doused
and hearts grown cold.
Come to comfort and cleanse
that we might be ready
to serve you once again
in the way and through the love
of Christ Jesus.   AMEN

STORMS

A gale swept down ... the boat was filling with water, and they were in danger.

~ Luke 8:23 ~

Waves crashing over our head,
feeling like we may go under any minute.
Buffeted and bruised,
wounded and frightened
by forces beyond our control,
or perhaps, in part, of our own making.

How do we respond?
Batten down the hatches?
Grin and bear it?
Keel over and collapse?
Retreat to safe havens?

We ride the storms of life,
utilizing coping mechanisms
learned and developed since childhood,
doing the best we can to survive.
And after the squall has passed,
once the swell has subsided,
what then?
As we draw breath,
in the lea of the wind,
gathering ourselves before we journey on,
can we pause and ask?
What have we discovered
about ourselves,
about others,
about God,
during the storm?

God,
Help us to be open
to learn from the turbulent times,
to grow with experience of helplessness,
to live through fear,
and not to seek to by-pass or ignore the pain.

Reading

Luke 8:22–5   *Discoveries through the storm*

Prayer Activity

Think of a stormy time in your life through which, in retrospect, you feel you have grown. Give thanks to God for what you have learnt about yourself, about how you relate to others or what you may have learnt about your journey of faith. These are discoveries may prove helpful for today or the future.

Prayer for the Church

Those who encourage and assist congregations to explore and develop patterns of life and mission appropriate to their own context

especially the Parish Development Fund Committee and the Scottish Churches Community Trust

Blessing

In the ups and downs,
In the storms and quiet times,
In my coming and going,
Sustain me,
O God.

Perceived

Perception means this: we are using our senses. Seeing, hearing, sensory input, data – all this information – it comes together at the point we call 'here'. 'Here' is where I am. 'Here' is where I take in impressions, and try to make sense of things.

And when I move, go from 'here' to 'there', I perceive differently. Things look different, reality *feels* different. And this is true as I move through time, too! Even from one place, a view, a panorama, constantly changes, with the play of light. I perceive things I didn't before. I lose other things in the mist or the shadows. I perceive grandeur because I am, in that place, small. I perceive mystery, because I am, in that place, unable to see everything clearly.

Here is where I am. Here is also *what* I am. I am not everywhere. I am not God. I am not exactly where you are. I am not you. Perception is to do with who I am, which is to do with *where* I am. Perception involves *seeing form here*. Perception involves perspective. A viewpoint.

The Gospel tells us that God's Word took flesh. The Church Father, Irenaeus, tells us that God the Son 'came and stood in a very small space'. Without ceasing to be God. The Creeds tell us that Jesus Christ was made fully human 'for us, and for our salvation'. Perception – the experience of being here, of only being able to see form here – in Christ, that is taken up into God. And so God understnads. We pray on the basis of our perceptions, from our perspective. And we are understood, in eternity.

HEIGHT

*Six days later, Jesus took with him Peter and James and John, and led them up
a high mountain apart, by themselves. And he was transfigured before them, and
his clothes became dazzling white such as no one on earth could bleach them.*

~ Mark 9:2–4 ~

Change happens in high places.
Fine wisps of air
bear and buoy the eagle;
the sun's radiance is captured
by the most frail of flowers;
and we become like children,
giddy and groping,
in the hanging, hopeful space
where heaven and earth collide.

From such a vantage point
it seems the pattern of my journey
weaves a wayward way,
turning to retrace well-worn
yet unfamiliar imprints in the sand.
Still on I scramble
heady and height-hopeful;
weary yet willing;
stretching for summits in my dreams.

For there are higher places still, Lord,
and my soul strives for them.
Perhaps one day my wandering steps will follow
till I, mesmerized by mountain mystery,
stand faltering but finally sure I've found only you.

Till then, help me not to lose sight
of your world at my feet.
And change me. Today.

Readings

Exodus 19:16–25   *God calls Moses to the mountain top*

Psalm 113   *The Lord is high above all nations*

Matthew 4:1–11   *The temptation of Jesus*

Luke 6:12–16   *Jesus goes the mountain to pray*

Prayer Activity

Where do you see God? Where are your 'transfiguration' moments? Pray about the places in your life and community that still reach for him. Pray for practical ways in which you and your congregation can reveal God there.

Prayer for the Church

As it meets in councils and assemblies to listen to God and one another

especially the Assembly Arrangements Committee, the Nomination Committee, the Moderator, the Moderator Designate, the Principal Clerk and the Depute Clerk.

Blessing

> Where hearts reach
> for heaven, Lord,
> send your blessing.
> Where souls strive
> for soothing, Lord,
> send your blessing.
> Where arms stretch
> for solace, Lord,
> reach down
> and lift us into your peace
> and your presence.
> Through Jesus Christ our Lord.   AMEN

MYSTERY

I shall lift up my eyes to the hills …
~ Psalm 121:1 (Good News Bible) ~

Where the clouds cluster around the hilltops,
Or the shadows fall across deep valleys,
Where thick canopies of leaves dapple a forest floor,
Or a dead-straight baked road across a dead-flat sweltering landscape
Shimmers away into the middle distance awash in pools of mirage,
                long before the gaze reaches the horizon,
It is difficult not to think of you, Lord.

Where there is a limit to vision,
Or a challenge to the mind's usually swift grasp;
Where I cannot instantly read what I see,
Or realize that what I saw is not what I first took it to be,
It is difficult not to think of you, Lord.

You are the God of mystery, dwelling in the thick darkness,
Beyond, so far beyond.

Mysterious landscapes there are, indeed;
Places where the senses' reach
gives out before the mind's grasp.
But what of where I am most of the time?
Just here. Or somewhere like it.
In the boring everyday …

Teach me, Lord, to know you
As the mystery of the unmysterious;
Filling the tedious landscape of the quotidian
with your presence.

If I have seen, in some mysterious place
A hint of you beyond what I can grasp,
Teach me that you are here, where life is lived,
Mystery at being's heart.

Readings

Genesis 28:10–22	*Jacob's ladder*
Exodus 19:16–25	*God speaks to Moses on Sinai*
Job 28	*Where does wisdom come from?*
Luke 4:1–13	*Jesus is tempted by the devil*
Acts 1:9–12	*The Ascension*

Prayer Activity

'Why is there something rather than nothing?' is a question that philosophers often frown on. Nevertheless, in the context of prayerful meditation, it opens up the most mundane surroundings to a perception of the mystery of being. Look around you, and dwell for a few moments on the mysterious 'thereness' of the place where you are – wherever it is, however mysterious or unmysterious, beautiful or unbeautiful you might think it.

Prayer for the Church

The organisations of women and men who worship, study and take the lead in reaching out to others

especially the Church of Scotland Guild.

Blessing

And God, to whom the mysterious places
Lift our hearts and minds in worship
Teach us his presence with us
As mystery at the heart of the familiar,
Gracious being, whose gift is being.

OPEN/CLOSED

Close your heart to every love but mine ... love is as powerful as death, passion is as strong as death itself.

~ Song of Solomon 8:6 ~

An awakening to possibility.
A noticing of another.
An impulse to give and share and enjoy ...
God you gave human hearts
to open and swell and surge
with powerful love.

So special the sharing ...
So amazing the feeling ....
So unspoken the trusting ...
So all-consuming the love that
Is too strong, too much.

God you gave human hearts
to open and swell and surge
with powerful love
and we close and restrict and limit
and condition and suppress and protect
our hearts that have been hurt.

So guarded the sharing ...
So painful the feeling ...
So broken the trusting ...
So devastating the love that
Is as powerful as death.

Easter God,
Bring healing and hope
Resurrection and restoration
to tightly closed hearts today.

Readings

Luke 19:18–30   *The rich ruler*
John 21:15–19   *Do you love me?*

Prayer Activity

Sit quietly for a while. Become aware of your breathing. Listen to and feel each breath, each heartbeat. Love and oxygen are both essential to life, similar in many ways but not the same. As you breathe easily and peacefully, think about the areas of your life where you love with ease and calm and rejoice for these times. Remember now, people and places where love is awkward and often a closed possibility, pray about these situations and ask God how things might shift.

Prayer for the Church

Those who steward the Church's financial resources and recall its members to the meaning of Christian giving

especially the Stewardship and Finance and the General Treasurer's Department.

Blessing

Open are the gifts of God,
Gifts of love to mind and sense;
Hidden is love's agony,
Love's endeavour, love's expense.

SURFACE

*... and they saw the God of Israel; and there was under his feet as it were
a pavement of sapphire stone, like the very heaven for clearness ...*

~ Exodus 24:10 ~

As I can run my fingers over some sensuous cloth
Or smooth, cool steel, or hard granite, or friable sandstone,
And enjoy the touch,
So I can run my eye over the velvet of a hillside
Or the sparkle of a choppy loch. Sight touches surface,
And stops there. *Depth* we must intuit.
We read it in, from contour. Or *used to ...*

Now, suddenly, for us, the look is all – and 'look' *means* 'surface'.
Suddenly, *all* is surface – ours is a *world of surface*.

And 'surface' might mean steel or polished stone,
or some unlikely steel-strong, stone-hard plastic. Or – glass ...
Windows now are walls! Glass lets those within see out,
But somehow – that's not the point! We, outside, don't see through, but look at
The shimmering surface ... glass – or steel, or polished stone, or plastic ...

Lord! If all is surface – where is depth?
If everything is outside, what is inside? And where are you?
And what are *we* but surface, now? Tattooed and pierced bodies wear,
Not clothes, but coded fashion-statements.
Was there ever a surface that humans *didn't* try to write on?

Yet you have always dealt in surfaces.
Happy to write your old covenant on the stones,
You write your new covenant on living hearts.
You scrawled your justice as graffiti
On Belshazzar's decadent wall.
Our names are graven on your hands.
the sign of your love is placed on our foreheads.
Teach us to read anew the Gospel of your love
Written on the surfaces of our world.

Readings

Exodus 24:9–18   *The surface on which God's covenant is enacted*
1 Samuel 16:1–13   *Surface and depth in God's reading of us*
John 8:1–11   *Dust, the erasable writing surface*
John 19, especially 1, 2, 18,
19, 22, 34, 37   *The inscription of God's passionate love*

Prayer Activity

Make a Möbius strip: take a strip of paper maybe eight inches long by one inch wide; hold one end steady and twist the other through 180 degrees, then stick the two ends together to make something like a link in a paper chain but with the all-important single twist in it. Now run your finger right along the outside of the strip – and see how the outside becomes the inside, then the outside again!

Why do we *need* 'inside' and 'outside'? *Does God?*

Prayer for the Church

Those who at all levels encourage and enable different branches of the Church to relate to and learn from each other and about the Gospel they share

especially the Committee on Ecumenical Relations and those involved in Action for Churches Together in Scotland.

Blessing

> *A man that looks on glass,*
> *On it may stay his eye;*
> *Or if he pleaseth, through it pass,*
> *And then the heaven espy.*

George Herbert

God give us to see through this world's surfaces
Not to the world's depth, but to creation's height.
God give us to look at the world's surfaces
And see written there the Gospel of his grace.

SACRED EARTH

God blessed them and said to them, '... have dominion over the fish of the sea and over the birds of the air and over every living thing that moves upon the earth.'

~ Genesis 1:28 ~

God
you have gifted to us this Sacred Earth
given to be co-creators
to look after it and to care for it

but now this sacred earth wails with fragility
through our lack of care, industrialization, greed and power.

So when we think that there is nothing we can do
Remind us of the difference
the tender touch of love can make.

So we will care for this earth
and try to live a more sustainable lifestyle
Feel its soil under our feet and know its precious goodness
Honour its people and creatures and treat them with respect
Listen to the rhythm of its heartbeat in sunset and season.

So when we think that there is nothing we can do
Remind us of the difference
It would make if we all did one small thing – today.

So help us Lord
To care enough to make a difference
So that we, and generations after us
Can still see the goodness of
this earth,
this sacred earth
Beautiful, gifted, fragile Sacred Earth.

Before time runs out.

Readings

Genesis 1	*Creation*
Genesis 15	*The promise to Abraham*
Psalms 8, 29, 33, 65, 104	*O Lord, how majestic is your name in all the earth*
Isaiah 65:17–25	*The new creation*
2 Peter 3	*The day of the Lord*
Revelation 21:1–8	*New heaven and new earth*

Prayer Activity

For each month, try to commit to doing one small thing that might make a difference to the earth – recycle, papers or bottles, turn of light bulbs, turn down heat, buy local food, use public transport, etc.

Prayer for the Church

Those who help us to take our place in, and be enriched by, the experience and witness of the Church throughout the world

especially the World Mission Council, Scottish Churches' World Exchange, and St Colm's International House, Edinburgh.

Blessing

Touch the earth lightly
Use the earth gently
Nourish the life of the world in our care:
Gift of great wonder,
Ours to surrender
Trust for the children, tomorrow will bear.

Serving Overseas with the Church of Scotland
with their families
(to be added to the Prayer for the Church for each day)

Day 1   ZAMBIA: Keith and Ida Waddell with Catriona and Mobita
Day 2   MALAWI: Helen Scott
Day 3   ZAMBIA: Colin Johnston
Day 4   ZAMBIA: Jenny Featherstone
Day 5   FRANCE: Alan and Lucie Miller with Jacob and Barnabas
Day 6   ISRAEL: Antony and Darya Short, with Joelle and Ezra
Day 7   TRINIDAD: John and Claudette Bacchas with Kerri-Ann and Shena-Marie
Day 8   ISRAEL:
Day 9   PALESTINE:
Day 10   BANGLADESH: David and Sarah Hall with Rebecca
Day 11   BANGLADESH: Helen Brannam
Day 12   BANGLADESH: James Pender
Day 13   SRI LANKA: John and Patricia Purves
Day 14   BERMUDA:
Day 15   BAHAMAS: Scott and Anita Kirkland with Priscilla and Sarah
Day 16   COSTA DEL SOL:
Day 17   ROTTERDAM: Robert and Lesley-Ann Calvert with Simeon, Zoe, Benjamin and Daniel
Day 18   ROME: William and Jean McCulloch with Jennifer
Day 19   AMSTERDAM: John and Gillian Cowie with Matthew, Sarah and Ruth
Day 20   LAUSANNE: Melvyn and Doreen Wood with Calum
Day 21   GIBRALTAR:
Day 22   GENEVA: Ian and Roberta Manson with Andrew, Robert and David
Day 23   BRUSSELS: Andrew and Julie Gardner, with Bethany and Karalyn
Day 24   MALTA:
Day 25   BAHAMAS:
Day 26   PORTUGAL: William and Maureen Ross
Day 27   HUNGARY: Aaron and Edit Stevens with Abel and Daniel

Acknowledgements

Scriptural quotations, unless otherwise stated, are from the *New Revised Standard Version*, © 1989 Division of Christian Education of the National Council of the Churches of Christ in the United States of America, published by Oxford University Press.

Pray Now 2009 was prepared by members of the Pray Now Group: Gayle Taylor, Carol Ford, Fiona Fidgin, Ewan Kelly, Tina Kemp and Owain Jones.

For further information about Pray Now and other publications from the Office for Worship and Doctrine, contact:

> Office for Worship and Doctrine
> Mission and Discipleship Council
> Church of Scotland
> 121 George Street
> Edinburgh EH2 4YN
> Tel: 0131 225 5722 ext. 359
> Fax: 0131 220 3113
> e-mail: wordoc@cofscotland.org.uk

We gratefully acknowledge Gayle Taylor, Tina Kemp and M. McGhie for their kind permission to reproduce the pictures used in this book.

Audio CD produced by Simon Jones Media.
Track 1 music © Simon Jones Media. Tracks 2–5 © Partners in Rhyme.